Waitre

A Supreme C

Published by Glowworm Press
7 Nuffield Way
Abingdon OX14 1RL
By Chester Croker

Jokes For Waitresses

These jokes for waitresses will make you giggle. Some of them you may have heard before, some you certainly won't and overall, this a huge serving of the very best waitress jokes and puns around. This book offers server jokes, serving jokes and waitress jokes in huge amounts.

These funny waitressing jokes, puns and gags are guaranteed to get you laughing out loud.

Published by Glowworm Press
7 Nuffield Way
Abingdon
United Kingdom
OX14 1RL

FOREWORD

When I was asked to write a foreword to this book I was very flattered.

That is until I was told by the author, Chester Croker, that I was the very last resort and everyone else he had approached had said they couldn't do it!

I have known Chester for many years and his ability to create funny jokes is amazing. He is an expert at crafting clever puns and amusing gags and I feel he is the ideal man to put together a joke book about our profession.

He is like us in that he can think on his feet very quickly, and I know he will be glad you have bought this book, as he has an expensive lifestyle to maintain.

May O'Naise

Table of Contents

Chapter 1: Waitress Jokes

If you're looking for funny waitresses jokes you've certainly come to the right place.

Here you will find both corny waitress jokes and original waitress jokes, all crafted to make you smile.

We've got plenty of great one-liners to start with, some quick-fire questions and answers themed gags, some story led jokes and as a bonus some cheesy pick-up lines for waitresses.

Chapter 2: One Liner Waitress Jokes

Here's one from an old movie to kick things off. The movie was called "Never give a sucker an even break" where the rude, sassy diner waitress Jody Gilbert says, "And another thing, don't be so free with your hands." to which W.C. Fields replies, "Listen honey. I was only trying to guess your weight."

In a country restaurant a customer said to the waitress, "Do you know whether the milk is pasteurized?" She replied, "Sure is; around here they run the cows out to pasture every morning."

There is a famous Cheers episode where Diane is being teased and she says, "You know, Sam, if I am to serve both as a waitress and the butt of jokes, I think I should make more money."

Carla weighs in with, "Yeah, what does a good butt make in this town?"

Confucius says a woman who looks to fortune cookie for advice will probably make a good waitress.

One for the kids - a waitress asks a teddy bear, "Would you like any dessert?" to which the teddy bear replies, "No thanks. I'm stuffed."

I got called pretty yesterday and it felt good. Actually, the full sentence was "You're a pretty bad waitress." but I am going to focus on the positive.

The cook flew into a rage at his new waitress saying, "Didn't I tell you to notice when the soup boiled over?" "I did," said the waitress, "It was 6:30 pm."

An old guy was shuffling in his seat before ordering his dessert of banana split to which the waitress asked, "Crushed nuts?" "No," he replied, "it's just arthritis."

My cross eyed waitress friend quit her job today.

She just couldn't see eye to eye with her customers.

You don't know the meaning of heartbreak until you see your waitress coming towards your table with food, but then veering off to a different table.

Classic put down:- She is so old, she was the waitress at The Last Supper.

A good sign you might be a Republican is you have ever called a waitress "Tootsie."

Two waitresses in a two person kayak were feeling cold, so they lit a fire in it. The kayak sank, proving that you can't have your kayak and heat it too.

I have never been in love. But I imagine the feeling would be something like the feeling you get when you see your waitress arriving with your food.

A sign outside a restaurant near me read 'Waitress needed - Must be 18 years old, with 20 years' experience.'

Did you hear about the restaurant on the moon? Great food but no atmosphere.

At a diner last week, I tripped and cut my leg and then the waitress fell on top of me adding in-salt to injury.

One for you music fans – "Waitress, there is a Flea in my Chilli Peppers."

Did you hear about the cannibal waitress who got disciplined by her boss for buttering up the diners.

A diner says to his waitress "Bring me something to eat, and make it snappy" to which the waitress said, "How about a crocodile sandwich?"

I asked my waitress whether service was included.

She replied, "It is not included but if you ask nicely, we might consider it."

Chapter 3: Q&A Waitress Jokes

Q: Where does a waitress wear a bikini?

A: In a breastaurant.

Q: What does a skeleton order when he is in a restaurant?

A: Spare ribs.

Q: What did the man say to his midget waitress?

A: You misunderstood me. I said I wanted shrimp for dinner.

Q: What is the difference between a piano and a tuna fish?

A: You can't tune a fish.

Q: What happened when a waitress crossed a hot chili pepper, a shovel and a Yorkshire terrier?

A: She got a hot-diggity-dog.

Q: Why was the Chinese waitress fired?
A: She was told to clean with spic-and-span, not spit-in-pan.

Q: What did the waitress say to the horse?
A: I can't take your order. That's not my stable.

Q: Why does the coffee taste like mud?
A: It was ground just a few minutes ago.

Chapter 4: Short Waitress Jokes

A waitress is struggling to find a parking space.

"Lord," she prayed. "This is maddening. If you somehow find a space up for me, I swear I'll start going to church every Sunday."

Suddenly, the clouds parted and the sun shone down on an empty parking spot.

Without hesitation, the waitress said: "Never mind Lord, I have managed to find one."

A blonde waitress meets up with a friend as she's picking up her car from the mechanic.

"Everything alright with your car now?" asks her friend.

"Yes," the waitress replies.

"Weren't you a little worried the mechanic might try to rip you off?"

"Yes, but he didn't. I was so relieved when he told me that all I needed was blinker fluid."

A panda walks into a diner. He orders a sandwich, eats it, then pulls out a gun and fires two shots into the air.

"Why did he do that?" the waitress asks her boss.

Her boss says "It's because he's a Panda. Look up Panda in an encyclopaedia and it will say. 'Panda. Large black-and-white bear-like animal that is native to China. Eats, shoots and leaves.'"

A waitress takes a man's food order.

"I'd like to get the turtle soup." he says.

The waitress places his order, but a minute later the man changes his mind and decides he wants the pea soup instead.

The waitress yells through to the kitchen, "Hold the turtle, make it pea."

A man in a restaurant, thinking no-one is around, lets out a very noisy fart.

The waitress glares at him, but he says to her "Stop that!" and the waitress replies "Sure, which way did it go?"

A young waitress is sitting at the bar after her shift, when a large, burly sweaty construction worker sits down next to her.

They start to talk and after a while the conversation gets on to nuclear war.

The waitress asks the construction worker, "Well, if you heard the early warning sirens go off, and you knew you've only got 15 minutes left to live, what would you do?"

The construction worker replies, "I am gonna make it with anything that moves."

The construction worker asks the waitress what she would do to which she replies, "I'm going to keep perfectly still."

A waitress brings the customer the steak he ordered, but she has her thumb over the meat.

The customer saw it and complained, "Why is your hand on my steak?"

The waitress replied, "I don't want the meat to fall on the floor again."

A waitress had a roofer called Gary working on her house repairing some tiles.

Gary is up on the roof and accidentally cuts off his ear, and he yells down to the waitress, "Look out for my ear I just cut off."

The waitress looks around and calls up to Gary, "Is this your ear?"

Gary looks down and says, "Nope. Mine had a pencil behind it!"

Three couples are on vacation and they are sitting down at a restaurant, and the waitress has just served their food.

The husband from Kansas says, "Could you pass the honey, honey" and his wife passes him the honey.

The husband from Oklahoma says, "Could you pass the sugar, sugar" and his wife passes him the sugar.

The husband from Iowa looks at his wife and says, "Could you pass the bacon, pig."

A waitress took her cross-eyed dog to the vet.

The vet picked the dog up to examine him and said, "Sorry, I'm going to have to put him down."

The waitress said, "Oh no! It's not that bad is it?"

The vet replied, "No, it's just that he's very heavy."

A waitress walks up to one of her tables in a Chicago restaurant and notices that the two Romanian men seated there are furiously masturbating.

She says, "What the hell do you guys think you are doing?"

One of the Romanian men says, "Ve arrre verrry hunggry."

The waitress says, "So how is whacking-off in the middle of a restaurant going to help that situation?"

The other Romanian man replies, "The menu says First Come, First Served."

A waitress calls up her local paper and asks "How much would it be to put an ad in your paper?"

"Three dollars an inch," a woman replies. "Why? What are you selling?"

"A six foot step ladder," said the waitress before putting the phone down.

A grey haired old man was eating at a truck stop when three members of a motorcycle gang walked in.

The first biker walked up to the old man and pushed his cigarette into his pie.

The second walked up to the old man and spat into his tea.

The third walked up to the old man and turned over his plate.

Without a word of protest, the old man quietly left the diner.

Shortly thereafter, one of the bikers said to the waitress, "Not much of a man, was he?"

The waitress replied, "Not much of a truck driver either. He just backed his truck over three motorcycles."

A man and his wife visit a steakhouse restaurant oblivious to the recent mad cow outbreak in the town.

The waitress tells them, "The specials today are salmon, halibut and roasted chicken."

The man says, "Well, I would like a sirloin steak done medium well."

The waitress replies, "What about the mad cow?"

The man replies, "She can order for herself."

A dog walks into a pub, and takes a seat at the bar. She says to the bartender, "Can I have a spritzer please."

The barman says, "Wow, that's awesome; you should join the circus.'"

The dog replies, "Why? Do they need waitresses?"

An obnoxious diner complained about the food he was given.

"Here," he said to the waitress, holding out a piece of meat, "do you call that a pig?"

"Which end of the fork, sir?" the waitress asked.

A customer wanted to ask his attractive waitress out on a date, but he couldn't get her attention.

Every time he caught her eye, she quickly looked away.

Finally he followed her into the kitchen and blurted out his invitation.

To his surprise, she consented.

He said, "Why have you been avoiding me all this time? You wouldn't even make eye contact."

"Oh," said the waitress, "I thought you just wanted more coffee."

Two lawyers were sitting down in a diner and they ordered two drinks.

They then produced sandwiches from their briefcases and started to eat them.

The waitress told them, "You can't eat your own sandwiches in here."

The lawyers looked at each other, shrugged their shoulders and then exchanged sandwiches.

Two chefs are having a conversation about sex in the kitchen.

The pastry chef says that sex is 75% work and 25% pleasure.

The sous chef says that sex is 25% work and 75% pleasure.

Not reaching agreement, they ask the waitress for her opinion.

The waitress says, "Sex is all pleasure."

The chefs ask her, "Why do you say that?"

The waitress replies, "Well, let's face it, if there is any work involved, I am the one who is doing it."

A guy looks over the menu in a restaurant, and after a few minutes, the waitress comes to the table and asks the guy what he'd like to eat.

"Well, I'd like a quickie."

The waitress blushes and says, "That's not funny, sir. Now, what would you like to order?"

"I'd really like a quickie."

The waitress slaps him and storms off angrily.

Another customer, overhearing the conversation, leans over and says to the guy, "I think you'll find that it's pronounced 'quiche.'"

A guy sits down in a restaurant and asks for the mushroom soup.

The waitress says, "The guy next to you had the last bowl."

The guy sees that the soup bowl is still full.

He says, "Are you going to eat that?"

The other guy says, "No. Help yourself."

He takes it and starts to eat it and after a couple of mouthfuls, his spoon hits something solid.

He looks down to see a dead mouse bobbing about in the soup, and he stops eating immediately.

The other guy says, "That's about as far as I got, too."

A waitress with one ear walks into a bar.

"Do you want a beer?" asked the bartender.

The waitress replied, "I've got one ear."

"What flavors of ice cream do you have?" the customer asked the waitress.

She answered in a croaky voice, "Vanilla, strawberry or chocolate."

The customer asked the waitress, "Do you have laryngitis?"

She replied, "No, just vanilla, strawberry or chocolate."

A waitress goes to the doctor with a hearing problem.

The doctor says, "Can you describe the symptoms to me?"

The waitress replies, "Yes. Homer is a big fat lazy man and his wife Marge is skinny with big blue hair."

Chapter 5: Waitress Stories

Diner: Waitress, this lobster's only got one claw.

Waitress: It must have been in a fight, sir.

Diner: Well, bring me the winner.

Diner: The crust on the apple pie was very tough.

Waitress: That wasn't the crust; that was the pie plate.

Diner: I thought the meals here were supposed to be like mother used to make.

Waitress: They are. She couldn't cook either.

Diner: There's something wrong with my hot dog.

Waitress: I can't help you; I'm a waitress, not a vet.

Diner: Waitress, I can't eat this meal.

Waitress: Why not?

Diner: I don't have a fork.

Diner: This fish isn't as good as what I ordered here last month.

Waitress: That's strange. It's the same fish.

Diner: Just look at this chicken. It's nothing but skin and bones.

Waitress: Would you like some feathers, too?

Diner: There's a button in my salad.

Waitress: It must have come off while the salad was dressing.

Diner: The portions are smaller than last time I dined here.

Waitress: It must be an optical illusion. The restaurant has been enlarged.

Diner: This food is repeating on me.

Waitress: We love repeat business.

Diner: Could I have a glass of water?

Waitress: To drink?

Diner: No, I want to rinse out something.

Diner: This bread is stale.

Waitress: It wasn't last week.

Waitress: I'm sorry to keep you waiting. Your soup will be ready soon.

Diner: What bait are you using?

Waitress: I'm sorry I spilt a glass of water on you.

Diner: That's all right. My suit is too large anyway.

Diner: What's this creepy crawly thing doing in my dinner?

Waitress: Oh, that one? He comes here every night.

Diner: This coffee tastes like soap.

Waitress: That must be tea, sir. The coffee tastes like mud.

Diner: My lunch is talking to me.

Waitress: Well you did ask for a tongue sandwich.

Diner: There's a fly in my custard.

Waitress: I'll fetch him a spoon sir.

Waitress: These are the best eggs we've had for years.

Diner: Well, bring me some you haven't had around for that long.

Diner: There is a cockroach on my steak.

Waitress: They will eat anything.

Diner: Send the chef over. I would like to complain about this disgusting meal.

Waitress: I'm afraid you'll have to wait; he's just gone out for dinner.

Diner: This coffee is way too strong.

Waitress: Best not to complain. You will be old and weak yourself one day.

Diner: Do you call this a three-course meal?

Waitress: That's right, sir. A pea, a mushroom and a tomato.

Diner: Have you got asparagus?

Waitress: We don't serve sparrows and my name is not Gus.

Diner: Waitress, is this soup kosher?

Waitress: What do I look like to you, a rabbi?

Diner: I am not very hungry; can I have a half portion?

Waitress: Sure. We never throw anything away.

Waitress: As you can see, we have pretty much everything on our menu.

Diner: I can see that; but can you bring me a clean one?

Waitress: What do you think about our restaurant?

Diner: I wish I had come by before.

Waitress: Why is that?

Diner: Your fish might have been fresh then.

Diner: Do you have chicken legs?

Waitress: No, I always walk like this.

Diner: This salad is frozen solid.

Waitress: That must be the iceberg lettuce.

Diner: This fish is very rude.

Waitress: It doesn't know its plaice.

Diner: This food is not fit for a pig.

Waitress: Sorry, I'll get you some that is.

Diner: This omelette is inedible.

Waitress: It's odd you say that. We have been making omelettes since you were born.

Diner: Then why are they not served until now?

Diner: Give me a hot dog.

Waitress: With pleasure.

Diner: No, with ketchup.

Diner: There's a frog on my plate.

Waitress: Yes - you ordered toad in the hole.

Diner: Why doesn't this restaurant have any specials?

Waitress: Because nothing about this restaurant is special.

Diner: I'd like a cup of coffee, with no cream.

Waitress: I'm sorry but we're out of cream. How about a coffee with no milk?

Diner: There's a dead fly in my wine.

Waitress: I warned him not to drink and swim.

Diner: Waitress, do you have frog's legs?

Waitress: Yes, Sir.

Diner: Then hop over here and get me the menu.

Diner: How long will the fries be?

Waitress: Normally, about five inches.

Diner: What's wrong with these eggs?

Waitress: I don't know; I only laid the table.

Waitress: How did you find your steak sir?

Diner: By accident. I just moved the tomato and there it was.

Diner: There's a fly in my ice-cream.

Waitress: Winter sports must have started early this year.

Diner: Two glasses of orange juice please, and make sure the glass is clean.

Waitress: Who of you wants the clean glass?

Diner: I would like a tray of sushi.

Waitress: Is that to eat; or to post photos of it on Instagram?

Diner: Do you serve crabs in here?

Waitress: Yes, we serve everyone.

Diner: Will my pizza be long?

Waitress: No; it will be round.

Diner: Do you have sausage and eggs on the menu?

Waitress: No, we clean our menus every day.

Diner: Why does the sign outside say "Fine Dining"?

Waitress: We can dream, can't we?

Diner: How come the Board of Health hasn't closed you down?

Waitress: They're afraid to eat here.

Diner: There's a wasp in my dessert.

Waitress: Yes, that's where they go in the winter.

Diner: Why don't you eat here?

Waitress: Serving it is cruel enough.

Diner: Why don't you have doggie bags?

Waitress: That would be cruelty to animals.

Diner: Why is this sandwich half eaten?

Waitress: I didn't like it.

Diner: Why are the servers in here so horrible?

Waitress: Just look at who they have to serve.

Diner: Why is there a spider in my glass?

Waitress: To scare away the flies.

Diner: There's a worm on my plate.

Waitress: That's not a worm sir, that's your sausage.

Waitress: If you know the food here is so bad, why do you keep coming back?

Diner: It reminds me of my ex-wife's cooking.

Waitress: Why are you taking so long to order?

Diner: I can't decide whether I want nausea or heartburn.

Diner: This soup is spoiled.

Waitress: Who told you?

Diner: A little swallow.

Diner: What is this cockroach doing on my ice cream?

Waitress: It looks like it is skiing.

Diner: There is a caterpillar in my salad.

Waitress: I'm sorry, I didn't realise you were a vegetarian.

Diner: There is a fly in the butter.

Waitress: That's a butterfly.

Diner: There is a spider in my wine.

Waitress: That's right. We've employed him to catch the flies.

Diner: Can I have a tooth pick?

Waitress: Unfortunately they are all in use right now. Can you wait five minutes?

Diner: What is in the soup?

Waitress: I don't think you want to know the answer.

Diner: Excuse me, but there is a hearing aid in my soup.

Waitress: Pardon.

Diner: This coffee tastes like dirt.

Waitress: That's because it was ground this morning.

Diner: I didn't order this.

Waitress: I know, but what you ordered tastes really disgusting.

Diner: What is this stuff?

Waitress: That stuff is bean enchiladas.

Diner: I know where it's been, but what is it now?

Diner: I can't eat this food, it's horrible.

Waitress: It's no good complaining to me, I wouldn't eat it either.

Chapter 6: Longer Waitress Jokes

A waitress was chatting to two of her friends about their teenage daughters.

Her first friend says, "I was cleaning my daughter's room the other day and I found a pack of cigarettes. I didn't even know she smoked."

Her second friend says, "That's nothing. I was cleaning my daughter's room the other day and I found a half full bottle of wine. I didn't even know she drank.

The waitress says, "That's nothing. I was cleaning my daughter's room the other day and I found a pack of condoms. I didn't even know she had a penis."

At a Mensa convention, several very intelligent members are at a local cafe and they noticed the shaker with an S on top, for salt, contained pepper and their pepper shaker, with a P on top, was full of salt.

They discussed how they could swap the contents of the bottles without spilling anything and using just the implements at hand and they finally came up with what they felt was a ingenious solution involving a napkin, a straw, and an empty saucer.

They called the blonde waitress over to dazzle her with their solution.

"Ma'am," they said, "we couldn't help but notice that the pepper shaker contains salt and the salt shaker contains pepper."

"Oh, sorry." she said. "Here, let me sort that out for you" and she simply unscrewed the caps of both bottles and switched them.

A man on vacation in Texas ordered an orange juice and a steak.

The waitress brought a pitcher of orange juice and the man's jaw dropped.

The guy said, "I ordered a glass of orange juice not a whole pitcher."

The waitress replied, "Sir, this is Texas. Everything is bigger here."

When the waitress brought a huge steak out the guy said, "Excuse me, I ordered a steak not a whole cow."

The waitress once again said, "This is Texas. Everything is bigger here."

After he finished his meal, the guy needed to visit the bathroom so he asked the waitress where it was.

She told him it was down the hall second door to the right.

However, he walked through the wrong door, and fell into a pool by mistake.

He yelled, "Help me, but whatever you do, don't flush."

Two waitresses were waiting in line in their bank late one afternoon, when some armed robbers burst in.

Some of the robbers proceeded to take money from the tellers, others lined the customers, including the waitresses, up against a wall, and proceeded to take their cash.

The first waitress jammed something into the other's hand.

The other waitress whispered, "What is that?

The first waitress replied, "It's your share of the tips from that party of 8 from earlier today."

A guy in a diner ordered a corned beef sandwich.

The waitress replied, "Sorry but corned beef sandwich is not on our menu. If you like I can give you our extra club sandwich which has some corned beef in it."

The customer asked what else was in the extra club sandwich and the waitress told him, "It is a double decker sandwich with tongue, corned beef, tomato, cheese, onion, lettuce and mayonnaise, all on sesame bread."

The customer told her he just wanted a piece of corned beef on white bread."

So the waitress shouts through to the kitchen, "One extra club sandwich. Make it one deck, hold the tongue, tomato, cheese, lettuce, onion, pickle and mayonnaise, and make the sesame bread white, untoasted."

An American cowboy was in a tea shop in England and he asked the waitress for her advice.

The waitress calmly said, "We recommend two types of tea, sir. The blackcurrant tea which is 90% substance and 10% aroma, or the peppermint tea which is 10% substance and 90% aroma."

The cowboy responded, "Well ma'am, where I come from, we have two types of tea too. There is s-h-i-T which is 90% substance and 10% aroma, and there is f-a-r-T which is 10% substance and 90% aroma."

The following gag should be read with an Italian accent.

One day I go to America and I stay in a bigga hotel.

I go down to eat soma breakfast. I tella the waitress I wanna two pissa toast. She bring me only one piss.

I tella her I wanna two piss; she say, go to toilet - I say, you no understand, I wanna two piss on my plate.

She say you betta no piss on plate, you sonna ma b*tch.

I don't even know lady, ana she calla me sonna ma b*tch.

Later I go to eata soma lunch the waitress she bring me a knife but no fock. I tella her I wanna fock – she tell me everybody wanna fock. I tella her, you no understand, I wanna fock on table. She say you betta not fock on table you sonna ma b*tch - I not even know lady ana she call me sonna ma b*tch.

I go back to my hotel room, an there's no sheet on my bed. I calla the manager and tella him I wanna sheet, he tell me go to toilet. So, I say, you no understand, I wanna sheet on bed. He say you betta not sheet on bed you sonna ma b*tch.

I don't even know man ana he call me sonna ma b*tch.

I go to check out of hotel and man at desk say peace to you. I say piss on you too, you sonna ma b*tch. I am going home to Italia.

Three waitresses and three waiters are ready to board a train to a convention. As they were in line to buy their tickets, the waiters noticed that the waitresses bought only one ticket between them.

The waiters bought their three tickets and boarded the train but watched the waitresses to see how they were going to manage with only one ticket.

As soon as the train left the station, the three waitresses moved from their seats and they all squeezed into one restroom.

Soon the conductor came through the carriage and knocked on the restroom door saying, "Ticket please." The door was then opened slightly and an arm reached out and the one ticket was handed to the ticket collector for him to inspect.

The next day, the waiters decided to do the same thing, and they purchased just the one ticket between the three of them. However they noticed that the waitresses didn't purchase any tickets at all.

They all boarded the train and as soon as the train left the station, the three waiters hurried to the restroom.

A few moments later, one of the waitresses got up from her seat, knocked on the restroom door and said, "Ticket please!"

Paddy and Mick are good friends and every night, they meet after work and have a drink in a local bar.

One day, Mick says to Paddy, "Paddy, if I die before you, promise me that you will have a beer for me, each day." to which Paddy agrees.

A couple of years later, Mick dies, and as he promised he would, Paddy has an extra beer for him every day after work.

This goes on for some time until one day Paddy comes in and orders just one drink.

The waitress is in shock, and says, "But, Paddy, aren't you going to have another drink for your friend, as usual?"

Paddy replies, "Well, the thing is, I joined Alcoholics Anonymous, but I don't think that Mick should be punished for that."

At a truck stop cafe a trucker and placed his breakfast order with a new blonde waitress. He said, "I want three flat tires, a pair of headlights and a pair of running boards."

The waitress went to the kitchen and said to the cook, "This guy out there just ordered three flat tires, a pair of headlights and a pair of running boards. Where does he think he is - an auto parts place?"

"No," the cook said. "Three flat tires mean three pancakes, a pair of headlights is two eggs sunny side up, and running boards are 2 slices of crisp bacon."

"Oh, OK." said the waitress. She then spooned up a bowl of beans and gave it to the customer.

The trucker asked, "What are the beans for, darling?"

The waitress replied, "I thought that while you were waiting for the flat tires, headlights and running boards, you might as well gas up."

Rebecca is talking to two of her friends, Julia and Sally.

Julia says, "I think my husband is having an affair with a waitress. The other day I found an apron bib under our bed."

Sally then confides, "Me too. I think my husband is having an affair with a hairdresser. The other day I found some scissors under our bed."

Rebecca thinks for a minute and then says, "You know - I think my husband is having an affair with a horse."

Both Julia and Sally look at her in complete disbelief.

Rebecca sees them looking at her and says, "No, seriously. The other day I came home early and found a jockey under our bed."

Chapter 7: Waitress Tales

Waitress tales:-"A customer once asked me 'Are you sure this is tea that I am drinking? It tastes like turpentine.' I replied, "It must be Sir, as our coffee tastes like gasoline."

Waitress tales:-"A customer once said to me 'I am not going to moan about the steak; but I cannot see that old horse any more that used to be tethered outside.'"

Waitress tales:- "A customer once asked me 'Can I have a tooth pick?' I replied, "Unfortunately they are all in use right now. Can you wait a minute?"

Waitress tales:-"A customer once asked me 'Have you got asparagus?' I replied, "I don't serve sparrows and my name is not Gus.'"

Waitress tales:-"A customer once said to me 'My cup is broken' I replied, "Don't worry. That just means that it is really good coffee."

Waitress tales:-"A customer once said to me 'There is a wedding ring in my soup.' I replied, "It belongs to the chef; let me know if you also find his finger.'"

Waitress tales:-"A customer once said to me 'There's dirt in my soup. What does this mean?'" I replied, "I don't know. I'm not a fortune teller."

Waitress tales:-"A customer once said to me 'Bring us a pitcher of beer every ten minutes until someone passes out; and then bring one every twenty minutes.'"

Waitress tales:-"A customer once asked me 'Do you serve crabs?' I replied, "Yes sir, take a seat. We'll serve anyone.'"

Waitress tales:- Thanks to being a waitress, I never want to have kids – or be an old person.

Waitress tales:- "A customer once said to me 'Why is my plate wet?' I replied, "It's not wet, Sir – that's the soup."

Waitress tales:- I was once told by my boss to try and push the soup du jour; as it was now a week old.

Waitress tales:- "Whenever I am serving an uptight vegan, I tend to walk on eggshells; which will really upset them."

Waitress tales:- "A customer once said to me 'Do you call this a three-course meal?' I replied, "Yes that's right Sir, a tomato and two peas."

Waitress tales:- "A customer once queried his bean soup to me, saying 'I don't care what it's been. What is it now?'"

Chapter 8: Waitress Pick-Up Lines

You are rare and well-done at the same time.

You brought me lunch, can I bring you dinner?

You're my missing ingredient.

You get 10 percent of the bill and 100 percent of my heart.

Can I sweep you off your practical, orthopedic waitress shoes?

Do you have any raisins? No? Well how about a date then?

Your body is about 65 percent water and I'm thirsty.

I have a big tip for you but you will have to receive it in private.

Since you are on your feet all day, do you want to lay down later?

Is work the only place that you are good at serving?

I cook best in the morning.

Guess what is on the menu. Me N U.

Chapter 9: Waitress Bumper Stickers

If you don't tip, stay home.

Tips should fold not jingle.

Beauty is in the eye of the beer holder.

Please don't seat them in my section!

Never trust a skinny chef.

I make serving food look good.

I like big tips and I cannot lie.

Chapter 10: Summary

Hey, that's pretty well it for this book. I hope you enjoyed this collection of waitress jokes. As you know, some were cheesy, but I hope they brought a smile to your face.

I've written a few other joke books for other professions, and these are from my electricians joke book:-

Q: What kind of van does an electrician drive?

A: A *Volts-wagon.*

Q: What do you call a Russian electrician?

A: *Switchitonanov.*

Q: What is the definition of a shock absorber?

A: *A careless electrician.*

About the Author

Chester Croker has written many joke books and has twice been voted Comedy Writer Of The Year by the International Jokers Guild. Chester is known to his friends as Chester the Jester and he has been in many diners and fancy restaurants in his time, which has provided him with plenty of material for this joke book.

If you saw anything wrong, or you have a gag you would like to see included in the next version of this book, please visit the glowwormpress.com website.

If you did enjoy the book, kindly leave a review on Amazon so that other waitresses can have a good laugh too.

Thanks in advance.

16476892R00044